The Magic School Bus Rides Again

Glacier Adventure

Adapted by
Samantha Brooke

Scholastic Inc.

Arnold

Dorothy Ann (D.A.)

Wanda

Carlos

Keesha

Ralphie

Jyoti

Tim

ISBN 978-1-338-25381-8

10 9 8 7 6 5 4 3 2 1   18 19 20 21 22
Printed in the U.S.A.   40

First printing 2018
Book design by Jessica Meltzer

Meet Ms. Frizzle!
No other teacher is like her. She takes her class on wild science field trips.

They go on her Magic School Bus. It twirls and whirls and can go *anywhere*.

Where will the bus take them today?

D.A. is practicing a story in front of Ms. Frizzle's class. But her story has too many facts and figures. The class is bored.

D.A. is supposed to tell the story at a **festival** tomorrow. "How can I wow everyone if I'm not a good storyteller?" she sighs.

Suddenly, Ms. Frizzle appears. "To tell a great story, you need to feel what you're saying. You need a story that's Earth changing!"

"The audience would love a story like that!" says D.A.

"Let's put practicing on ice and find you a story," says Ms. Frizzle.

The Magic School Bus turns into an airplane. Ms. Frizzle and the kids fly away.

"Wow, look at that **glacier**!" shouts Carlos.

"What's a glacier?" asks Tim.

"It's a river of ice that only forms on land and is always on the move," says D.A.

"Let's go see the glacier up close," suggests Ms. Frizzle.

"Wahoo!" the kids shout. They turn into snowflakes and float to the ground.

"This is not on my permission slip!" cries Arnold.

The kids land on the glacier, and the bus lands on top of them.

"I feel like an ice-cream sandwich," says Carlos.

"That's how glaciers form! They are built layer by layer out of snow, ice, and stuff that sticks to the ice, like dirt," Ms. Frizzle explains.

"I wonder how many snowflakes it took to make Earth's glaciers," D.A. says. "Can I use the bus's **calculator**?"

"I don't think the bus has enough power for that math. We need all our power to climb the glacier," answers Ms. Frizzle.

"Ms. Frizzle, the math will be so cool," pleads D.A.

Ms. Frizzle agrees. But the calculator uses up all the bus's power!

Suddenly, the wheels stop moving. Uh-oh . . . now the bus is sliding down the glacier!

"Aaahhhh!" everyone screams.

The bus skids out of control.
When it finally stops, only
D.A. and Ms. Frizzle
are there.

"Where is everyone?"
D.A. cries.

"Let's find them,"
says Ms. Frizzle.

Ms. Frizzle calls Ralphie and Carlos on a walkie-talkie.

"Welcome to 130,000 years ago!"

"We went back in time?" asks Ralphie.

"No. The ice has air bubbles from the past trapped inside it. Those air bubbles can tell a very interesting story," Ms. Frizzle says.

Suddenly, magic bubbles fill the air. They take the boys back to 130,000 years ago.

"Whoa, we're cavemen," says Ralphie. "And there's a saber-toothed tiger. Cool!"

"Not cool! He looks hungry," cries Carlos. "Run!"

The boys' adventure ends just in time.
"Look at all this **data** from the ice!
I even know the **temperature** from
130,000 years ago," D.A. says.

Next, the magic bubbles take Jyoti and Arnold back to 20,000 years ago.

"This guy walked here from the other side of the world because the ocean was so low," says Jyoti.

"Did he bring lunch with him?" groans Arnold. "Anything is better than this."

Afterward, D.A. tests the air bubbles from 20,000 years ago.

"The temperature has only changed a little between the first time and the second one. I wonder what will happen next," she says.

The magic bubbles take the kids to find Tim in the year 1800.

D.A. tests the air. "It's not much warmer now than it was 20,000 years ago. Wild!"

"Too wild!" says Carlos. "We have to get out of here before that volcano blows!"

Next the magic bubbles take the kids to find Keesha in the year 1970.

"No saber-toothed tigers here. Just cars, factories, and wacky clothes," Keesha says.

D.A. is busy doing **research**. "These numbers are crazy! In the last 170 years, there has been a huge temperature rise."

Finally, the magic bubbles take everyone back to Wanda, who's waiting on the glacier.

"Does the data show that it's warmer now than it was in 1970?" D.A. asks.

"D.A., be careful over there. It looks like the glacier is melting," Wanda says.

Suddenly the ice breaks and Wanda falls!

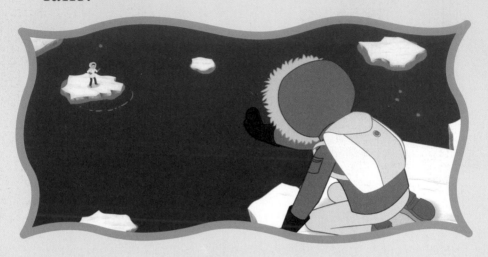

"Hang on!" cries D.A. She tosses down a rope, but she's not strong enough to pull up Wanda.

"Ms. Frizzle, help!" cries D.A.

The bus quickly pulls Wanda to safety.

"Wait, where's my tablet?" D.A. asks. "It has all my data. I can't tell my story without it!"

"Sorry, D.A. It's time to go back," says
Ms. Frizzle.

"But my story is trapped in the ice,"
says D.A.

"Then we'll take the ice to go, like
scientists do. We'll drill down and get a
core sample," says Ms. Frizzle.

Back home,
it's almost time
for the festival.
D.A.'s parents,
friends, and lots
of other people
are there.

"My story is going to
amaze you," she tells them.

"I hope she talks about more than
numbers this time," Wanda whispers.

"What was Earth like 130,000 years ago? This ice core sample from a glacier is going to tell the story with me," D.A. begins.

"Bus, do your stuff!" she continues. The bus shows pictures to help D.A. tell the story.

"Long ago, there were woolly mammoths and saber-toothed tigers. Back then, the weather was warmer and there was more water in the oceans," says D.A.

"But then Earth got colder and more ice formed. More ice means less water in the oceans. It stayed like that for thousands of years," says D.A.

"Around 200 years ago, we started
making cool stuff like planes and cars
and factories. But some of these things
make smoke and **gases** like **carbon
dioxide** that go into the air," says D.A.

"These gases trap the sun's heat and keep it close to Earth," D.A. continues. "This caused the temperature to get warmer. Ice started melting, which added more water to the oceans.

"The temperature has changed more in the last 200 years than in the 100,000 years before that.

"If things keep going this way, Earth is going to get even warmer. Some places will get more rain and **floods**. Other places will get hot and dry, with less foods and fewer kinds of animals.

"But that's not the end of this story," says D.A.

"If we don't like the way things are going, we can do something about it! Everyone can help by doing less of the stuff that makes these gases.

"Kids can help, too. We can walk or bike instead of taking cars everywhere. We can turn off lights and computers and plant trees," says D.A.

"And we can share the story glaciers tell us. We can work together to give this story a happy ending for the glaciers — and for us," says D.A.

The crowd cheers — D.A. wowed them!

She told a great story that was full of facts. And it had lots of feeling, too.

Professor Frizzle's Glossary

Hi, I'm Ms. Frizzle's sister, Professor Frizzle. I used to teach at Walkerville Elementary. Now I do scientific research with my sidekick, Goldie. I'm always on an adventure learning new things, so here are some words for you to learn, too! Wahooo!

calculator: an electronic device that answers math problems

carbon dioxide: a gas that is produced when certain fuels are burned

core sample: a piece of material that is taken from Earth using a special drill, and then examined

data: facts or information

festival: a special time or event where people gather together to celebrate

floods: large amounts of water covering areas of land that were formerly dry

gases: substances like air that have no fixed shape

glacier: a very large area of ice that moves slowly across land

research: a careful study that is done to report new knowledge about something

temperature: a measurement that indicates how hot or cold something is